D0386350

Letters to Mead

By Peggy Mulvihill
With Introduction by Susie Mulvihill Parran

Sourcebooks Inc.

Naperville, Illinois

Copyright © 1995 by Peggy Mulvihill and Susie Mulvihill Parran
Cover Design © 1995 by Sourcebooks, Inc.

Published by: **Sourcebooks, Inc.**
P.O. Box 372, Naperville, IL 60566
Phone: (708) 961-3900; Fax: (708) 961-2168

"The Falling Star" reprinted with permission of Simon & Schuster, Inc. from *Collected Poems of Sara Teasdale*. Copyright 1930 by Sara Teasdale Filsinger, renewed 1958 by Guaranty Trust Co. of N.Y.

Excerpt in 8-21-92 letter, © Flavia Weedn 1995. All rights reserved. Any reproduction of this work or portions thereof without written permission of the copyright proprietor is expressly prohibited.

Excerpt from *All Rivers Run to the Sea*, by Joyce Hifler reprinted with permission of Doubleday, a division of Doubleday Dell Publishing Group, Inc.

Excerpt from *The Little Prince* by Antoine de Saint-Exupery, copyright 1943 and renewed 1971 by Harcourt Brace & Company, reprinted by permission of the publisher

Mulvihill, Peggy
     Letters to Mead : for anyone who's ever loved a child / by
Peggy Mulvihill ; with introduction by Susie Mulvihill Parran.
        p.   cm.
     ISBN 1-57071-052-X (hc)
     1. Mulvihill, Peggy, date—Correspondence. 2. Mulvihill, Mead James,
1952-1967—Correspondence. 3. Mothers—Correspondence. 4. Mothers
and sons. 5. Parenting. I. Title.
HQ755.8.M85   1995
306.874'3'092 — dc20   95-23997
                                                                          CIP

Dedication

This book is dedicated with love to the memory of
Mead J. Mulvihill III, to my husband, Mead,
and to our other three extraordinary children
David, Bob and Susie

*Softly falls the snow
and as it does...The bleak ground
awakens in white.*

*Haiku by
Mead J. Mulvihill III,
1952–1967*

Preface by Peggy Mulvihill

When I began writing letters to my first born, I was really doing it for my own enjoyment. I thought it would be fun in my golden years to be able to look back on those very special days. Somewhere in the ensuing years, I thought that they could become an "interesting" gift to the children when they reached their 21st birthdays. The children all knew that I was writing them, and they knew that they couldn't read them until they were 21. Only David gave me a hard time about that. I mention his frustration with me only because of his reaction when he finally received his packet of letters, tied with a ribbon and given to him with his parents' love. If you're lucky, once in your lifetime you will see your children almost speechless with gratitude. We were lucky enough to see it two more times after David. With tears in their eyes and looks of gratitude on their faces, they all accepted these gifts. Looking back on it now, if I had a choice of giving them the letters or a fancy, sleek convertible, I'd go with the letters.

It was at those times that I decided some little angel had put the idea into my head. From "letter day" on, each of our children knew without a shadow of a doubt that they were appreciated, that they were loved. That is the beauty of this gift and the reason I agreed to share it with the world. You can be the poorest person in the world, and you can put together this gift. My children will tell you that the letters were written on all kinds of note paper, tablet paper, whatever was handy at the time.

Purists will tell you that my sentence structure is often faulty; my punctuation leaves much to be desired. The only thing that it has going for it is pure, *unadulterated love—and that's what parenting is all about. Making children feel loved seems to make very fine citizens of this universe.*

Thank you for reading our book. It has given us an opportunity to leave more footprints in the sand for Mead J. Mulvihill III.

Introduction
by Susie Mulvihill Parran

How do you thank someone for giving you the gift of life <u>and</u> the gift of a lifetime…?

My mother, Peggy Mulvihill, has always had a way with words, delighting us with poems and journal entries on family vacations and, together with my father, instilling in my brothers and me a love of the English language.

Her most special gift, however, was the writing of our birthday letters. Each year, for each child, she would compose a loving epistle chronicling the year's progress: personality traits, sibling relationships, milestones, special moments, even world events. We knew that she was writing them, but we weren't allowed to read them until our 21st birthday. On that day, she would hand to us the stack of 21

1

letters, wrapped in love and a ribbon.

When my brother died from the Asian flu at the age of 15, I assumed that his letters had been put into the coffin with him. Since I was only 6 years old at the time of his death, my memories of my oldest brother were frustratingly few and far between.

Imagine my delight to learn last year that his letters were safely tucked away in a box under my parents' bed. (A letter _had_ been put into the coffin with him, but it was one Mom had written after he died.) I was so excited! I planned to read one or two letters a night, to savor the experience of getting to know the sibling I had lost. But the letters were so compelling, the too-short life of the extraordinary child who was my brother so poignantly told, that I kept reading...and reading....The hours passed in a moment as the life of a bright and gentle young man came

2

too soon to an end. But I realized, in reading these letters, that the spirit of Mead still lives in all of us (that I even share certain traits with him!). As Thomas Campbell wrote, "To live in hearts we leave behind is not to die."

And it suddenly became very important to me to share Mead's life—these letters—with a larger audience. I want the world to have the incredible privilege of knowing my big brother, Mead James Mulvihill III.

Thank you, Mom, for so lovingly chronicling the moments and milestones that make up a child's life…for providing a history that enabled me to know the brother I was too young to remember…for allowing me to share his story with others…for the lifetime of love that you and Dad have given to Mead, David, Bob and me.

"From the very first you've been an extremely alert and intelligent child. (And it's not just your very prejudiced parents who think so.) Show you how to do something once or twice and sure enough you'd up and do it for us, then squint your eyes and laugh."

August 13, 1953

Dear little Mead,

For your first birthday I would like to set down on paper the record up to now.

One year and three hours ago (6:50 a.m.) you became a statistic—one more citizen in a world troubled by the turmoils of a war in Korea. You preceded by almost three months a fiery election in which a very great man— Adlai Stevenson—was defeated for President.

But since this isn't a record of world history, rather, a record of your history, we'll get down to facts.

You weighed in at 6 lbs. 3 oz.—19 inches long. The consensus of opinion was that you looked very much like a little sparrow. Your features, tho', were perfect and,

5

since you gained weight rapidly, you were a very handsome young chap in a very short time. As a matter of fact, at a month you were considered too pretty to be a boy.

We were astounded when we took you home (to our apartment at 5551 Centre Ave) to find that you were an exceptionally good baby. The books had prepared your daddy and me for a little monster that would keep us pacing the floor all night long. You didn't! One night you had us up from midnight to two a.m. because you had stuffed yourself with too much milk and it kept backing up on you. As a matter of fact, you did a powerful lot of spitting up until you were nine months old—probably because you always ate more than your little tummy could hold.

Around four months your back, leg and arm

muscles had developed unusually well. You were always pulling yourself up to a standing position. At seven months you started walking a few steps around your playpen. At eight months you were going like lightning around tables, etc. You could've walked by yourself by ten months but you continued holding onto things more for moral support than physical. A week before your first birthday Hilda got you to let go and you really stepped out. No crawling after that. You were so pleased with yourself that I think you'd have walked twenty-four hours a day if we'd have let you.

People, too, were amazed at how well you were grasping the talking idea. Practically everything started with a "b" or, if it didn't, you made it. For instance, when you see a dog, you shiver with excitement and joyously yell "bog, bog!"

One of your first words, and first loves, was

"book." Others on your list include bird, bye-bye, button, bottle, etc.

The first year brought no illnesses, nary a sniffle (and I still knock on wood). You've been an extremely healthy and happy child.

At ten months you finally got four teeth and right now you're working on a fifth. Even with this affliction of the very young, you've been an angel.

From the very first you've been an extremely alert and intelligent child. (And it's not just your very prejudiced parents who think so.) Show you how to do something once or twice and sure enough you'd up and do it for us, then squint your eyes and laugh.

Daddy and I are particularly pleased with your love of music and sense of rhythm. You dance to all music, including singing commercials. As I've said

8

before, you love books, but you also love flowers. A very cultured young gentleman you are. If the first year's progress as a child is any indication of the end product of the man, then you're slated to be quite a guy. Daddy and I are sure that's what the future will hold. We look forward to each day and year of watching you develop. We'll give you everything we can that we feel is best— moral and material. We feel sure that you'll have the innate intelligence to grasp the qualities we so hope you'll possess—tolerance, honesty, decency and all the others that go to make a "real gentleman."

If you ever read this you might wonder why it was written. I can only answer that it is more for my satisfaction than your enlightenment. We—your daddy and I—love you very much and are terribly proud of you and happy with you. In twenty years I think it will give us

9

much happiness to read the first year's record of our first son and heir.

Happy birthday, baby.

Love,
Mommy

August 13, 1954

Dear little Mead,

 Another year has just flown by—a year peppered with the Army-McCarthy hearings, the appointment of a very great man, California's Governor Earl Warren, to be Chief Justice of the United States, and a very humane and just decision by that body to end segregation in the whole United States. All of this is very important, generally, to all of us. But most important, particularly, to your Mommy and Daddy, has been watching you grow and develop.

 Two weeks before your first birthday we moved into our own home (5470 Fair Oaks St.). We all loved it, but I think you probably appreciated it most of all. The

11

backyard is a delight to you, particularly during the nice weather.

We all thought you were going to be an early talker, but pretty soon I got the suspicion that, maybe after all, that didn't fit into your plans. It's characteristic of you to be absolutely certain of a thing before you do it. Notice I said "do it," not "try it." Daddy and I have become so adept at interpreting your sign language that you get every single idea across without so-called "words." The only words you bother with are Dadda, Momma, goggie, key, book, ball, truck and suitable noises for trains, fire engines, food, etc.

Some people think it's too fantastic to believe, but it's true. You're a positive joy to take places or just to be with at home. I don't think in two years that we've been out without you more than a dozen times. I took you to *see the Ice Capades when you were fourteen months old. Everyone thought I was daffy to attempt such a thing. They were sure I'd have to leave by the end of the first number—at the latest. You loved it. We had to leave at the middle of the show to pick up Daddy at law school and it made you miserably unhappy to be dragged away.*

You loved the children's zoo last September, on your first visit, and you love it even more this summer.

Daddy and Uncle Noble took you to see the trains one Saturday and then to look at new cars and couldn't get over how wonderfully well you behave on outings. Of course, Daddy and I frequently take you to the club for dinner and you're always a perfect little gentleman. You first went out to dinner, to Sodini's, with me a couple of days before your first birthday.

Christmas was wonderful and we have movies

13

which tell the story better than I could report it.

On Valentine's Day we got our dog, a Boxer—whom we promptly named Valiant, Prince of Pilsen—Val, for short. He was wonderful with you and you with him and the friendship between you is growing stronger each day. There have been, of course, minor happenings but nothing serious.

You still love flowers and books, but this year we'll add cars to the list. You have quite a fleet of them down in the dining room. When Daddy's home, the two of you divide the time reading books and racing your cars, trucks, fire engines, etc., back and forth from living room to dining room. It's funny, but when a daddy has a little boy, a mommy suddenly discovers that Daddy is really a little boy at heart. I often watch the two of you and envy that oneness of mind you share.

On the subject of health and happiness, you're both healthy and, apparently, happy. One day you seemed slightly under the weather and I took your temperature. It was 102 degrees. I called Dr. Quinn and he came up to examine you. It turned out that you had a slight sore throat and the beginnings of a cold. He prescribed Aureomycin and, tho' we stayed indoors for five days, you didn't get sick at all. Even during those five days, tho' I was prepared for, and would have understood, some trying moments, you were an absolute angel. Never once did you fuss.

On July 5th (the day the 4th was being observed) I took you to the Isaly's on Walnut Street to get milk and cold cuts. You were standing beside me leaning against the cooler when your feet slipped and down you went. I thought you'd just received a slight bump but when I

picked you up the woman behind us gasped that you were
bleeding. You sure were. They gave me ice in a towel and
soon I had slowed down the blood and stopped your
crying. I brought you home and Daddy and I washed the
gash and put Merthiolate on it. Then we called Dr.
Quinn. He was away for the weekend but Dr. Scurletis
asked me to bring you to the Emergency Room at
Pittsburgh Hospital. I did. Dr. Scurletis asked me to leave
the room while he took stitches in the cut. I didn't want to
leave but I realized that it would be easier for you and me
if I weren't in the room. I stepped outside and when you
started to cry—as who wouldn't—I thought my throat
would explode. I thought of the old saying, "It hurts me
worse than it hurts you." When my mother used to say it
when I was a little girl, I always thought that she was
lying. How could she hurt at all when I was the one

16

*having the pain. Now I know how she felt and someday,
when you're a daddy, you'll know what I mean. Your
daddy and I felt both stitches—and more. We felt the
agony of helplessness and our great love and concern,
faced with not being able to prevent the hurt, is an
experience neither of us wants to face very often. The
unhappy part of that fact is that we realize full well that
there will be many times that we'll be faced with that
problem—both hurts of the body and hurts of the heart and
mind. Happily, you seem to be a rare creature who listens
to that much shunned "voice of experience." May God
give you the gift of keeping that gift as you grow older.*

*Another gift that you possess is rarely found in an
adult, much less a child. Needless to say, I hope it's a
virtue you'll always have. You're almost fanatical about
cleanliness and neatness. You love clothes—and dislike*

*getting them dirty. You also dislike dirty hands. You're
extremely careful—for a child—about keeping your toys
in somewhat reasonable order. And you love to keep doors
and gates closed—much to the consternation of poor Val.*

*Daddy has to work at KQV tonight so we had a
small birthday celebration at noon. Elizabeth and Penny
walked over to have some ice cream and cake with us.
You seem to be happy with all the clothes and toys
Mommy and Daddy gave you, but you're especially
pleased with the Ridem Locomotive. It's really
heartwarming to give you presents, no matter how large
or how small, how few or how many.*

*You're very pleased to get something to wear or
play with that belonged to your mommy or daddy. I'm
going to save some things of yours and hope that one day
your child will also treasure them.*

It's about time for you to awaken from your nap and then we'll be off in Cabby's convertible for another birthday celebration at Grandmommy's and Granddaddy's.

I'll close the pages of the second year by reminding you that Mother and Daddy love you very much. We cherish great dreams and hopes for you and somehow know that you're the kind of little guy that completely justifies our dreams and hopes.

Happy Birthday, honey.

Love,
Mommy

P.S. As a matter of record—on your second birthday you're working hard on all four (2 year) molars, but you're not causing us any trouble. You did have a bad hour or so at the club a few Sundays ago, but gee, everyone's entitled to a bad day now and then.

P.P.S. Also for the record—you're beginning to come along very well on the toidy idea. That's the only thing concerning you that I felt almost hopeless about.

> We love you very much,
> Mommy and Daddy

January 1, 1955

My dear little Mead,

Happy New Year, Son. Many things have happened since I wrote less then five months ago. You're growing up so fast that I thought it best to split the year and record your history in two parts annually.

You're growing up in the "jet age," the "A and H Bomb age." Your parents wonder "what's to become of us—of civilization?" As nearly as I can tell, tho', parents have been asking that question of themselves and others for many centuries.

Daddy and I seriously wondered, as we grew somewhat philosophical last night, about the galaxy, the speed of the earth circling the sun, the strangeness of it all.

21

Perhaps by the time you are a young man a practical space ship will have been made—perhaps by then we'll know whether there is life on any other planet. The jets of this age are fantastic to behold. The steps of progress made in air travel in just these past two years is enough to take your breath away. Yet I know that when I read this in ten or fifteen years, jets will probably (as far as we know them) be childish and outdated.

There are many points of history I'd like to record here—the shift to the Democratic party once again in this past election, a man named "Dr. Sam" Shepherd found guilty of murdering (2nd degree) his wife and sentenced to life. If this decision stands, he'll be paroled, most likely, when you're 22 years old. (To set the record straight— I'm still convinced of his innocence.)

However—this is your history, my pet. You are still

such an angel that it's hard to believe any child could be so good. Right now as I write, you're trying your best to interest me in playing one of your games. You're really starting to talk now and the sound apparently delights you.

Christmas was terribly exciting for you this year. You're now the very, very happy owner of a fire engine, a tricycle, a wonder horse, a gasoline station, a blackboard, numerous new books and a heap more. You were appreciative of everything you received. You accepted each gift as if it were the loveliest in the world. There's nothing quite like the joy and delight of a child at Christmas— unless it's the joy and delight of the parents.

One thing happened to mar a perfect holiday season. You and I took Val down to Dr. Glenn's this morning and had to leave him there for a few days. You were awfully sweet to him. Giving him kisses and patting his head as if to make the hurt go away.

Shortly after your second birthday, and without telling anyone of my plans, I took you to see your first movie—Walt Disney's "Vanishing Prairie" at the Squirrel Hill Theatre. You were an awfully good little tyke and you just didn't want to leave when it was time to go.

The same thing happened at the flower show when we went with Laurie and her mommy. You were entranced by all of the beautiful flowers and birds and cried a bit when we left.

We had great fun beginning about the first of September when we started taking Val to Schenley Park. While the swings were up, they were your chief form of entertainment at the park. When they took them down you turned out to be a great little hiker. You were mad for walking knee deep in leaves through the woods.

Sometimes there were other children to play with, sometimes you enjoyed just rolling down the hills, playing ball with me or Val, or just sort of exploring all by yourself.

When you decided to start on the toidy, that was that. Since your second birthday, I don't think you've made a mistake more than four times.

All in all, your daddy and I are very, very, very pleased with you. We couldn't have wished or planned a more perfect son.

All our love,
Mommy

"*Already you're smart enough to have figured out that being young and little is just about the nicest thing in the world.*"

August 13, 1955

Dearest Meadio—

    It's a fantastic day and age we're living in. The "Atoms for Peace" plan is beginning to take shape and the Lord only knows what modern conveniences will be available in the next few years. Even now, living is far simpler than our ancestors ever dreamed it could be.

    In this year of '55, the world lost perhaps the greatest scientist of all time—Albert Einstein. The world found a great humanitarian right here in Pittsburgh—Dr. Jonas Salk. Thanks to his untiring efforts the world will probably be greatly relieved of the dreaded disease, polio.

    Great things, and things that are sometimes not so great, are constantly happening around us. Today, however, something pretty nice is happening right here in our home. Impossible as it seems, today, young man, you are three years old. For some reason—until your first gift arrived—this didn't appeal to you in the least. Already you're smart enough to have figured out that being young and little is just about the nicest thing in the world. Mr. and Mrs. Blumenthal brought your birthday present—a huge set of drums—over last night and you're now quite thrilled with the niceties that accompany a birthday celebration.

Your "mommio" and "daddio" are still quite thrilled with just about everything you do. You continue to be a healthy and happy little twerp and, generally, as well behaved a child as any parents could hope for. Because of this, we were totally unprepared for your behavior in Atlantic City this past week. The first morning Daddy and I took you for a walk on the beach and your new tennis shoes—of which you were very proud—got wet and dirty. After that you didn't give us a minute's peace. You wanted to go home and told us so every two minutes.

You were also quite lonesome for your "big big goggio" and told us that on alternate minutes. Two days after we got there Mommy got sick, so the next morning your wish was granted—we packed up and started for home. You were bubbling you were so happy. You've been your sweet little self ever since. This much we can say for our vacation. You're a great little car traveler. You didn't sleep for a minute either way but you never gave us a second of trouble. When asked why you don't like Atlantic City now, you're frank to admit that "It's all wet there."

Something else rather exciting is coming up. If all goes well, a playmate will arrive for you around the 19th of February. Things haven't been as smooth for Mommy this time as they were with you, so I hesitate to be definite about it. But, God willing, you may have a brother or sister (I'm betting on the latter) to share toys with. We're slightly anxious about your reaction to this interloper but have our fingers crossed that you'll continue to be as sweet as you are now.

At long last you're beginning to talk so that people other than your mommy and daddy can understand you.

As far as TV, you're an avid Ding Dong School and Circus fan.

You have an aversion to ponies—real or merry-go-round type. Though you love to look at them and read about them, you point blank refuse to ride on them.

Yep—one of your first loves is still books. As you can imagine, this pleases Daddy and me no end.

You have a passion for milk and fruit. Naturally, you also eat a normal amount of other foods.

You're a big fellow and a handsome one. But the things Daddy and I are most proud of is the fact that you enjoy a reputation of being a neat, clean and especially well-behaved little boy.

It's no wonder we're proud of you and love you so much. Just stay as sweet as you are and you'll be the most popular guy in town.

Much love from—
Mommy, Daddy and Val

"All in all, you're quite a little guy.
You call us a 'happy family.' We are,
honey, an extremely happy family."

February 24, 1956

Dear Meadlet,

Since August 13th, 1955 many things have happened—most important of which is the fact that you've become a "big brother." But to keep things straight let's take things in order.

In late August, you found a pal—Jeff Grier. Our jaunts to the park became more frequent and lasted much longer because you and Jeff loved the woods, the ponies, the buckeyes, the swings, the running and the exploring. Jeff's mommy and I—and, of course, Val—loved it also. We were a very unhappy quintet when the weather prevented further excursions. But we still visit back and forth with Jeff and we're anxiously awaiting the coming of

33

spring and many more visits to the park.

After much "just looking" at ponies you finally decided in late September to ride. "Buckskin" was the first and is still the favorite.

We had fun on Halloween—you were a monkey; I, the organ grinder. Christmas was, as always, a big delight. You asked Santa for two things: a chewing gum truck and an Indian hat. Since you've been such an angel all year (except for the Atlantic City episode) Santa naturally brought you both and much, much more.

At about this time, the birth of your baby brother was getting close and you were delighted with the idea. Daddy and I thought we'd not have any problems with you—tho' we were warned to the contrary—and we were oh-so-right. You have been just perfect. You can't do enough for your little brother. And I mean it when I say that you've honestly been a big help in caring for David.

Your talking is beginning to shape up real well now. And, though the talking has been slow to develop, nothing else about you has been slow in the least. Your mental ability and agility amaze Daddy and me.

Your social manners are excellent. Your understanding and patient behavior with other children of all ages is a sight to behold. We are really and truly as proud as proud can be.

You stayed up to watch Peter Pan a few months ago and we've been on a Peter Pan-Captain Hook-Indian kick ever since. You have three favorite TV shows: Ding Dong School, Children's Corner and Rin Tin Tin. Howdy Doody, Fury and Circus you also like but otherwise you can take TV or not—usually, and I think preferably, "not."

That just about brings us up to the half year

mark—except…

You decorated your own room in November. You picked the furniture, the drapes, the bedspreads, etc., and you did a magnificent job. You're as pleased as punch with your job but I think that Daddy and I are even more pleased.

All in all, you're quite a little guy. You call us a "happy family." We are, honey, an extremely happy family. I don't think the future could hold anything but good things for such a good little fellow. Daddy and I often stay awake until the wee hours of the morning discussing you, and now your little brother, and wonder what the future holds for all of us. Only time will tell, of course, but things look awfully rosy from our perch of 1956.

We love you, baby.

Love,
Mommy

August 13, 1956

Dearest Meadie,

Where the time has gone? I don't know, but today you are four years old. In the year of your birth, Adlai Stevenson was the Democratic nominee for President. Today, the Democratic convention opened in Chicago. Stevenson and Harriman will fight it out—ballotwise—later in the week.

A few weeks ago the Italian liner, Andria Doria, sank off Nantucket.

Six months ago your baby brother was born.

Yesterday you had your first birthday party. A good time was had by all.

But at this time, you are the important one. You

have grown to be a gentleman of whom we are very proud. Except for being athletically inclined, you are very like your daddy. We won't push you into any profession, but we're going to be rather surprised if you don't follow your two namesakes into the legal profession. Your mental gymnastics in logic have us amazed.

Your ties to parents and home are rather evident at this time. You are violent in your assertions that you don't want to go to school and you will not get married. You're resigned to the fact that you must go to school, but that doesn't make you like the idea.

You had a great springtime romance this year— Kim Gebron. She's been in California for over two months and you miss her very, very much.

Your brother, David, loves you so very much and you love him just as much. You help me take care of him and play with him when I'm busy.

All in all, my sensitive little bunny, we're so proud of you that words just can't express it. You're the very nicest kind of son and we love you very much. Stay as sweet as you are.

All our love,
Daddy and Mommy

$41^{1}/_{4}$ inches tall
39 lbs. 12 oz.

"Daddy and I can't help but be eternally grateful that God gave you to us. You've been a source of more joy and happiness and inspiration than you could ever know."

August 12, 1957

My dearest Mead,

    Tomorrow you will be five years old. It comes
as a bit of a shock to me because I can remember so
well the day I wrote my first letter to you on your first
birthday.

    The events (historically) of the past year all
seem dwarfed by something that happened to you. You
were baptized at St. Paul's Cathedral on January 14th
of this year. David was baptized at the same time. Aunt
Reed Havey and Bob Grigsby are your Godparents and
Aunt Cabby and Uncle Ed Havey are David's. Ten
days after you became Catholics, your daddy was also
baptized and received into the church. Your Godmother

and David's Godfather were Daddy's sponsors. It's been
a thrilling experience for me and I know that one day
you'll realize why it stands out in my mind as the event
of the year.

As for this—your fifth—birthday, it was
celebrated yesterday with a party that was a humdinger.
Your guests included: Jeff Grier, Kim and Julie Gebron,
Ricky and Cindy Ross, Jeremy and Jeff Gibbs, Carole
and Ellen Burstein, Skip Olson and Seth Kreimer.
You had such a wonderful time. True to form, you've
been thanking me all day and telling me how much fun
you had.

You haven't changed much in this past year. You're
still thoughtful, considerate, lovable (very lovable) and
more than a little dependent on your mommy and daddy.
We sent you to nursery school at Dr. Quinn's insistence

42

and you were doing pretty well until you came down with a series of colds that kept you from school for about seven weeks. After that you didn't want to go back. Dr. Quinn relented since there were only five weeks of school left, but we now face the same battle this year because you seem to be thoroughly opposed to kindergarten, too.

Unless I go to birthday parties with you—or any place else for that matter—you won't go. It's both flattering and exasperating. But giant strides are being made now and I think you'll change by next year at this time.

We went to Cape May this summer and, in general, had a magnificent time. The first few days were rough because you lost your balance in the first ten minutes we were on the beach and fell down in very shallow water. So—you wouldn't go back in. We reasoned with you, tried force and bribes but to no avail. You never went into the water again during our week's stay. Both Daddy and I were afraid of the water as children, too, though, so I guess you come by your fear honestly. When we wised up and stopped trying to get you into the water, you had fun and so did we.

We have a family where I think the key word is love. You're so sweet with David, who just adores you. We all love each other very much and I think that even you and David can feel it. Perhaps you don't know how to label it but you feel the goodness and know it's here.

Daddy and I can't help but be eternally grateful that God gave you to us. You've been a source of more joy and happiness and inspiration than you could ever know. To date, you've more than fulfilled our happiest *dreams. Thank you for being so sweet.*

You've always been crazy about cowboys and Indians, but between the age of four and five it's been a particular passion. Strap on your holster, pull on your boots, slap a cowboy hat on your head and you're ready to challenge the whole world.

I have a maternal instinct which says that, with or without the cowboy getup, you'll always meet any challenge that this old world will offer. Not in a loud, boisterous way, but rather with a sane, sensible and well-thought-out approach which rarely misses.

Dave has a big brother to look up to who can't help but teach him the difference between the right way and the wrong way. Mommy and Daddy are happy about that and Davey Poo is, too.

Stay as dear and sweet as you are. It's going to be a rewarding experience to watch you grow and develop into manhood.

Happy birthday, Son.

Love always,
Mother

January 7, 1958

My dearest Mead,

So many things happen when you're five that one letter from August 13th, 1957 to the same date in '58 just isn't enough.

My dear little boy, without realizing the magnitude of recent events, you go along playing cowboy as if everyone who ever lived was part of the "space age." It's breathtaking to consider the possibilities of the life you'll lead when you're a man. Russia has launched Sputnik I and II and we view the heavens with a new curiosity. What is up there—when will we know? I feel sure that you and your generation will be a vital part of it. I hope that with our new knowledge we will also realize a rebirth of love for our fellow man.

You have a tremendous curiosity, something which I hope will never be stifled. You certainly show more than a passing interest in science—the sun and the moon and the stars. Perhaps one day it will be your field. If so, I hope that you will contribute to a lasting peace—not just a temporary calm.

Whatever your profession, Daddy and I feel sure that in you there's a great deal worthy of contributing to our society. You're a wonderful son and a wonderful person.

Your aptitude for learning astounds us. You play Tic-Tac-Toe and we can't beat you. You're now learning to play checkers. On your own you're learning to add, subtract, read and write. But, with kindergarten you're bored silly. You tolerate it because I threatened to get a job if you didn't go.

You're an understanding winner and an extremely gracious loser. In games of chance like Bingo, Candy, Lassie, etc., you don't get impatient or upset in the least if you lose. Your concentration is fantastic for a five year old.

A few weeks ago—four, to be exact—you were chosen to be crowned a prince by King Friday XIII of Calendarland (Children's Corner). It was such an exciting day and we were all so very proud of you. I know of no one more worthy of being called "Prince"—but, then, perhaps I'm a bit prejudiced.

You got an American Flag for your birthday and how you love getting it out for holidays. The day before Yom Kippur you came home from school and said, "Tomorrow's a holiday but we have to go to school, so will you put out the flag for me, please?"

Before your Christmas vacation, you came home and asked me if I knew that little Jewish children didn't celebrate Christmas. I said, yes I knew. Then you said, "They have something called 'Hanukkah'—that's how they celebrate Christ's birth." Without knowing it, on both occasions you gave our neighbors a couple of good chuckles.

Christmas in '57 was bigger than any other. Before Christmas you gave away hundreds of toys to children less fortunate than you. Santa and everyone else was so pleased that your gifts were bigger and better than ever. To coincide with the space age, you got a missile launcher, a sky sweeper, a satellite launcher, a supersonic car, etc. But, because little boys are still little boys, you got a bow and arrow, a new rifle, a tool kit—just like Daddy's—Winnie The Pooh, a book which you just adore, and an electric football game.

Now that the frantic of Christmas is past and the cold weather has <u>really</u> come, you and David are learning how to ice skate. Nothing could please me more. After ten years, I finally have an excuse to go ice skating again.

You and David are still great buddies. You are absolutely dear with him. And he, of course, idolizes the ground you walk on. It's no wonder that Daddy and I are so proud and pleased with both of our boys.

What do we hope for the future? Well, there's not much left to hope for except that you stay as sweet as you are. Certainly you have small faults—or at least they seem now to be faults. You prefer being here with us, so you won't go to parties or even visit your friends without us. This, I'm sure, you'll outgrow all too soon. But for the great part we couldn't ask for a sweeter little guy. God has been good to your daddy and me. We don't take that fact for granted. We are eternally grateful for you, our treasured gift from our God.

We love you, Son, with all of our hearts.

Mommy

August 19, 1958

My dear little Mead,

Six days ago you reached the wonderful age of six—a milestone in your young life.

In a few weeks you'll start school. Though you've been to nursery school and kindergarten, this will be a completely new experience for you. Now you'll go all day and now you'll begin to learn the written word in earnest. You have your doubts and you've voiced them. Believe it or not it takes a peculiar kind of inner strength to pretend that your doubts are a little foolish. You see, I still remember well my first day in the first grade. I was a terrified, lonely little girl who couldn't understand why my mommy would force me to leave home and familiar toys and people. I guess every parent must die a little at this first token gesture of cutting the apron string and yet each of us knows that it must be done. I think that in time you'll love school because your mind is a curious mind. It grasps greedily for knowledge. Thank God !!!

But to get back to past events. You had a birthday party last week that was another humdinger. It was a pirate party and your eyes danced and glowed like stars when you saw the table. There were pirate hats and pirate flags, daggers and treasure chests, and, best of all, a magnificent cake baked in the shape of a pirate ship. Then there was a treasure hunt for shiny new pennies. You and your little guests had a wonderful time.

We had a wonderful time on our vacation this year, too. You and David made your first flight on an airplane. What a glorious experience for a little boy *almost six. You loved every single second of it. We arrived in Cape May and, because of last year and your aversion to the ocean, Daddy and I didn't know quite what to expect. We needn't have worried, though. Our only problem was keeping you out of the water. And on some days when the water would reach a record low of 55 degrees we couldn't understand how you and David could do more than get your big toes wet, but out into the deep waves you'd charge and so we'd tag along. But it was great fun and you proved once more what a marvelous, marvelous gift we received when you were born to us.*

You took another big step in the past six months. You finally started going to parties, movies, etc., with your little friends and I no longer had to tag along.

David adores you and most of the time you're very sweet with him. You have your share of frantic arguments about whether a soldier is yours or David's—small things like that—and you've become a little bit of a tease where Dave is concerned, but all of this, I'm sure, is quite normal. David is, after all, at a very exasperating age. We all have our "sit on David" moments and he needs it. But with you as an example I'm sure that he'll be a pretty spectacular little guy, too.

In the next four or five months, we'll have another brother or a sister for you. We only pray that our luck holds out and that he or she will be the joy that you and Dave have been.

Now and as you grow older there will be many times when you wonder how much we love you. Times when you want something so much that it would seem unfair not to have us give it to you. Believe me, darling, though our acts may or may not be wise acts, all we want in this world is your happiness. Happiness involves a great deal more than material things and Daddy and I hope that you'll understand and know that our love for you is an undying love. It's a love that directs our every action.

And so, my son, another year has whizzed by. A year of toy soldiers, books, rockets, boats, airplanes and games. A year when you've decided it's unmanly to cry. A year when you've given me a few gray hairs and an untold number of smiles. We love you, little one— very much.

Kisses and Hugs,
Mommy

P. S. Just recently you've met one of your idols—Josie Carey. You had a Coke with her the other night and walked hand in hand down the street with her afterwards. You're mighty glad Daddy's doing "The Greeks Had A Word For It." In the near future Josie will be here for dinner and you're the envy of your Tame Tiger friends.

February 28, 1959

Dear Mead and David,

On January 21st Granddaddy Mulvihill died. He became ill two days before but by Wednesday he was in a great deal of pain and, after collapsing, was taken to the hospital. David and I picked you up at school that day and Dave could hardly wait to tell you that Granddaddy had been taken to the hospital in an ambulance. You asked me if that was true and I told you that it was. So as not to alarm you I cheerfully said, "They think they're going to have to remove Granddaddy's appendix. You know, like David had his tonsils removed." In a very solemn little voice you said, "Well, you know, Mommy, Granddaddy's getting old and you've got to expect that he's going to die." I scolded you and warned you never to say such a thing again.

Daddy was at the hospital, so you and Dave and I ate in the kitchen and then you two boys went down to the gameroom to play. There were many phone calls but you never came upstairs. Then Daddy called and told me that Granddaddy's chances were not good. That it wasn't a ruptured appendix but rather a ruptured aorta and that they were performing "heroic surgery." When I hung up the phone you came upstairs and said, "That was about Granddaddy, wasn't it?" I said that it was. You said, "He isn't going to live, is he?" I said that we hoped he would. Then you said, "He isn't going to, Mommy, he's going to die." Two hours later he did die.

The next morning I told you that Granddaddy died the night before and you said, "I told you he was going to, Mommy" and I agreed that you had. Then you absolutely shocked me by saying, "What was wrong with Granddaddy? Wasn't he getting enough blood?" Of course, that was just about it. Your next statement was, "Don't worry, Mom, Granddaddy's in Heaven with God right now."

We, of course, felt the same way but it was comforting to have you verify it.

Even you, Dave, with the wisdom of one very young, had an opinion. When Grandmommy O'Brien showed you Granddaddy's picture in the paper, you remarked, "You know, he up and died on us!" As truth would have it, we all sort of had that feeling. We all felt as if we had suddenly been deprived of our leader.

I hope, boys, that you'll never forget your grandfather. You loved him and he loved you—very much.

Mommy

"Is it any wonder that all who knew and loved him [Granddaddy Mulvihill] felt a little empty, a little lost when God saw fit to take him from us."

February 28, 1959 (12:02 A.M.)

Dearest Mead, Dave, and Bobby,

How does one write a eulogy for a great man? How does a mother capture on paper the personality of her sons' grandfather? This is my labor of love in the wee hours of this morning.

On January 21st—your birthday, Dave—Granddaddy Mulvihill died. The memory of Granddaddy Mulvihill has not. He was a remarkable man and a loving grandfather. His career in law was brilliant. He was a lawyer's lawyer. In his early days he was one hell of a pilot. But, most of all, he was a man who was loved and respected by all kinds of people—governors, truck drivers, judges, newsmen, big businessmen, household maids. His time and best efforts belonged to each of them and all of them. He was a man of honor—a man of his word. Even those who were on the opposite side of the fence respected him, trusted him.

Thousands of people paid their last respects, many grown men knelt by the coffin and wept. When he died he took a little of each of us with him, but, typically, he left a lot of himself with us. Untold numbers had been helped by Dad in every conceivable way. Is it any wonder that all who knew and loved him felt a little empty, a little lost when God saw fit to take him from us.

I hope, Mead, that you'll remember Granddaddy. He thought you were such a smart little guy. He was so proud of you and loved you so much. Possibly even you, David, will have some recollection. I hope so, because I think you were kind of the apple of his eye. In you he saw *himself. And I think he was right: I think you will be very much like him. Again—I hope so. You, Bobby, can't possibly remember that he held you and loved you as he loved your two brothers. He couldn't bear to hear you cry. As with Mead and David, he'd eat his dinner with one hand or not even bother to eat, just so you could be held and made happy. I hope that you can get a feeling—though I'm not adept at expressing myself—of the kind of man who is part of you. He was not a plaster saint, but that's all to the good. He was human, and I hope that each of you possesses some small part of him—his human and humane qualities.*

Life goes on for us and, through us, for Granddaddy Mulvihill. Your heritage is greater because of him. Love him always. He'll be with you in planes, on the football field, in court, wherever you are, whenever

you need him. His grandsons were his pride and joy—
he'll not forsake you.

Love,
Mommy

August 13, 1959

Dearest Mead,

Can it possibly be time to say "Happy Birthday" to you again? It must be, honey, because you're so grown up these days.

We had your birthday party on Sunday (August 9th) and it was a dilly. Flying and airplanes are the passion and bywords around here these days so, naturally, the theme of our party was airplanes. TWA gave us posters and Allegheny Airlines provided Junior Pilot and Junior Hostess wings. We hung little airplanes from the chandelier, had airplane pencil sharpeners and airplane candy baskets for favors. Two hundred balloons, an airplane cake, and the U.N. flags finished off the decorations. It was very colorful and very gay—a fitting celebration for a young man of seven.

As I mentioned, you're rather mad about airplanes. Daddy's taking lessons, so you and David are often found at Campbell's airport crawling around the planes or being "cranked" around the field. The whole house is evidence of this phase of your life. We've got more airplanes, books on airplanes, etc., lying around here than you could ever imagine.

You have other interests. You collect baseball cards and are now awaiting the football cards. You still like to walk in the woods, read books, swim in our pool, go to Kennywood, play Croquet, and dozens of other things.

In the past few weeks you've calmed down a lot, but six was sometimes a troublesome age. You never bullied anyone younger than yourself—or even the same age—but I understand that you provoked a few fights with older boys. It was an age where you experimented a few times with lying out of things but it didn't work and I think you've given the idea up completely. We had to be a little rough on you at times but we understood that you had happened upon the first _really_ independent year and you had to challenge the world. You clashed head on with the time-tested fortress of social customs and requirements. There are many other things for a bright young boy to challenge and conquer and, to your credit, you seemed to grasp this fact almost immediately.

Ours is a happy family, honey. Though it's sometimes frightening to realize the great responsibility we have in raising you boys, it's a responsibility and a challenge that we wouldn't trade for anything. We hope that the very great love we have for you and Dave and

Bob will counteract any mistakes in judgment we may make when raising you to manhood. You're three pretty spectacular little guys, to our way of thinking, and we're sure that you'll be the same kind of men.

When I wrote last year, we were expecting another baby. Now Bobby is eight months old and you love him very much. You don't pay as much attention to him as you did to Dave but there's no doubt that you think he's awfully nice.

I expect that you may be quite a ladies' man. You're very popular with the girls now and, so far, you seem to think they're pretty nice, too. The big crush this year was on a cute little girl named Katie Clarke.

All of this is incidental in your young life. The main thing is that you're a happy, healthy little guy—

loved by your daddy, mommy and two brothers. We think you're a great little boy.

> All my love,
> Mommy

"Everyone in the operating room came down to tell us how good you'd been and how they'd never had anyone—man, woman or child—who had asked such intelligent questions while waiting for the operation to begin."

November 10, 1959

My dear little Mead,

At ten o'clock this morning you were wheeled up
to the operating room for a herniotomy. From all reports
you conducted yourself in your usual deliberate and
intelligent ways.

You've been a brick through it all. You came into
the hospital two days ago, and though you're in a private
room and I fully expected to stay, you'd have none of it.
You even tried to talk me into going home tonight, tho' I
found out later it was for my sleeping comfort that you
suggested it and you were really happy—you said—that
I'd stayed.

For two days you've pretended that you were on a business trip—like Daddy—and with all your new games, etc., you had a ball. But the motto for today is, "I don't feel a bit well." You've had slight discomfort, though you'd punch me if you knew I'd used the word "slight." You did mention that you wished the operation hadn't been today. When we asked you when you wished it would be, you answered, "Two years ago!"

I gave you a puppet—Harry Horse—last night before I went home, to keep you company. When I called bright and early this morning to tell you Mommy and Daddy were on their way to the hospital, you said that Harry insisted on going to the operating room with you. Hours later—after a shot designed to dope you up—you still chattered about Harry insisting on going, so the nurse took him in the crib with you. When you were wheeled

down from the recovery room at noon, you were clutching
Harry for dear life. He was, and has been all day, indeed
a friend in need.

You have been, my dear little boy, a son to fill his
parents' hearts with pride. That so small a frame carries
so much courage and heart around inside it is almost
inconceivable. We're so proud of you we could burst—
and justifiably so.

Ten minutes after you were back in the room this
morning you were coloring a map of the United States.
And tonight you had made us promise we'd go to Open
House at Wightman. Once again we were bursting with
pride. You're one of a few leading the class with no mark
under 100% since school opened. What a little guy!!!

As I look over at you now, my sleeping angel, I
thank my lucky stars that you're ours. We couldn't have

asked for a sweeter, smarter, braver, wiser or better little boy.

Rest well, baby, and know that we love you very much.

Mommy

P.S. Everyone in the operating room came down to tell us how good you'd been and how they'd never had anyone—man, woman or child—who had asked such intelligent questions while waiting for the operation to begin. You, however, have insisted that you didn't behave well at all. When pressed for your reason for saying this, you confess that you cried for me in the recovery room. I still think you were mighty, mighty good.

Dr. Shiring says that maybe you'll come home on Sunday. Golly, will poor little lonesome David ever be glad to see you!

August 13, 1960

My dearest Mead,

The other evening you said to me, "I'm awfully glad I was born. Sometimes I wonder if I'm not just having a long dream it's so nice!" Truly, honey, a parent couldn't hear nicer words. But you have nothing on us— we're awfully glad you were born, too. You've brought a bushel of happiness to Daddy and me.

This past year has been a wonderful one for you. You've really broken out of the cocoon. You have dozens of friends and you have a decided loyalty to them. You have a newfound, very passionate love—baseball. You're the soaring spirit of boyhood—a challenge to life itself. Little boys, I'm sure, are what give the world hope. In you I can see and sense and almost taste an unchained enthusiasm for life and living. In this past year, there's been a feeling of world tension that seemed to anticipate an all-out nuclear war. Perhaps it will happen one day or perhaps our prayers will be answered. I have greater hope that at least a semi-peace will exist because of little guys like you.

Many words have been written about little boys—imaginative words, descriptive phrases. Certainly I can't compete with these great authors, but as the mother of three sensational sons, I feel that little boys somehow seem to have a rapport with the whole world. I think, perhaps, that my favorite subject in the whole world is little boys. Somehow a house filled with the sounds of little boys is not a noisy house—just a comfortable, happy house.

Since your seventh birthday you've been a busy guy. You managed to snare an all "A" report card for the

year from Miss (Rhoda) Phillips, one of the most superb
teachers I've ever encountered.

You had a hernia operation from which you
made a rather rapid recovery. The day after we brought
you home from the hospital I found you standing on
your head. Dr. Shiring, who performed the operation,
unfortunately has died since.

You've managed to accumulate enough
information and facts on baseball to become an authority
on the favorite pastime of our country. Of course, I
hasten to add that this is natural enough because seven
year old boys are authorities on all subjects.

This is the year that you barely tolerate girls.
Except for Andi, Julie and Kim, whom you just can't
escape, you prefer the company of David Meyers or Jack
Twersky or one of the other boys.

You still like airplanes and your first love—
reading—is still one of your favorite pastimes.

I've noticed one decided difference between you
and our David. It may be the age or it may be different
personalities: you're the steady, thoughtful, sometimes just
slightly pessimistic one. David is the gambler, the more
impulsive of the two. You've been a doll with Dave. You
haven't shut him out of your life. He's a very mature,
able little guy strictly because of his relationship with you.

And so, my dear Meadie, it's time once again to wish
ya' a happy birthday. May you continue to grow physically
and mentally as tall and beautiful as the most stately poplar.
You're quite a boy, my son, and we love you very much.

Hugs and kisses,
Mom

Essay by Mead circa 1960

My Brothers
by Mead J. Mulvihill III

My little brother, Bobby, once spilled a bag of toys. My mother made me clean it up.

My other brother, David, calls peas "beans." David doesn't know what "artificial" means. My mother told him some flowers were artificial. He said, "Put 'em in water."

Bobby sat down a while and watched me write this note about my brothers, but Popeye came on so he watched it.

I once had to stay in. I went to Brodie's to see if

they had David. David was not there. I called my mother. She said, "Go back to school." On my way back to school I saw Gerrie Shapiro. She told me that David was at school. I found him there waiting for me.

David loves to watch commercials. David loves bubble baths. So does Bobby. Bobby has a kiddie cart and David likes to ride it.

Bobby has a Playschool garage. He stuck his head in it, then he took it out and laughed.

David likes me to read books to him.

Bobby likes to eat cookies. After Bobby eats he keeps his bib on.

David wants to write a note to Santa to ask to be an elf.

David learned to swallow a pill before I did.

Bobby likes to play with typewriters. And Bobby likes to crawl up on the dining room table.

Sometimes they're pests, but I love them anyway.

Merry Christmas
from MEAD

"You were born to inherit the space age and somehow I feel a lot more confident knowing that your generation will be masters of this age."

August 13, 1961

My dearest Mead,

At best, it comes as something of a shock to realize that I'm the mother of a <u>nine year old</u> boy. Happy Birthday, honey.

Since the days when I wrote my first letters to you, you've come a long way and so has this crazy world. You were born to inherit the space age and somehow I feel a lot more confident knowing that your generation will be masters of this age. Already our first astronaut has been sent into space. Shepard first, and just last week, Gus Grissom followed. Perhaps Glenn will be the first American to circle the earth. But someone your age—or perhaps a few years older—will probably one day land on the moon or Mars. You have a mind peculiarly geared to science and space but you've made it plain that good old terra firma is for you. I wonder! Will your ideas change as you get closer to the wildly courageous, positively fearless teens. You're attending classes at Buhl Planetarium's Junior Space Academy this summer mainly because your mind—just as when you were an infant—grasps passionately for new knowledge. Your light is somewhat hidden under the proverbial basket because you are still just a bit on the shy side and it would never occur to you to show off.

Lest you read this in a quarter of a century and conclude that you were the "studious kind," let me try to present the whole picture. You are a well-rounded young man. If ever there was a passionate love affair, it's between you and the national pastime—baseball. Your first comment or question in the morning and the last at night is almost certainly going to pertain to baseball. You received your birthday gift from Grandmommy Mulvihill early this year—a week at the National Baseball School. Among others, you were instructed by Bill Virdon, Roberto Clemente, and Bob Friend of the Pirates, and Roseboro of the L.A. Dodgers. I have never seen you enjoy anything so much.

For our vacation this year, we spent eight days with the Brodies at Hickory House in Jennerstown. You, my little nature boy, had the time of your life. You swam and fished and hiked and tried to fight back tears when the time came to leave. All in all, it's been a pretty fabulous summer for you.

To get back to your favorite subject I might add that, since your last birthday, you also had the thrill of seeing the Pirates win the Pennant. We were at that seventh game of the Series—you and I—and what an unforgettable day it was. We even joined in the horn honking and confetti throwing that went on in Oakland that night.

You did well in school this year and we pray that this statement can be made every year. I think you'll be buckling down to a more advanced kind of learning this year and I'm anxious to see how you fare.

This year you, David Meyers, Mark Perlis and Jack Twersky started a little science club. You usually met at our house and it actually gave me a thrill to watch my budding little scientists in action. Miss Alpert—your teacher this year—was quite impressed with the sincerity with which the four of you approached this and with the results that ensued.

88

Your closest baseball companions were Marty Blumenfeld and David Meyers. Your two chess companions were Fritz and Jeannie Lindauer. And your best friend during those periods when you had to get away from competition and just <u>relax</u> and enjoy life was and is Andi Brodie.

The nine years we've had you, Daddy and I have loved you more than life and respected you more than you'll ever know. You are worthy of every bit of that love and respect. Every parent feels—I'm sure—that his child or children are something special. We don't ask that you must set the world on fire but we do hope that you'll try. Because as long as you "try" and conduct yourself according to the (it's corny, but true) Golden Rule, you'll be a success. Even if your name never makes the history books—even if you don't have a million dollars in the bank—you'll have the love and respect of your parents, your brothers and sister, your wife and children, your neighbors and, truly, my dear son, no man can be a greater success than the man who possesses this.

We love you,
Mom

August 22, 1962

My dear Mead,

Nine days ago you reached your tenth birthday—a rather frightening thought for your parents who feel much too young to fully comprehend this fact or to understand where the years have gone.

It's been quite a year for you. When you returned to school last year (September '61) you found out that you'd been put into the advanced 4th grade. Shortly thereafter you were asked to join the Creative Writing Club and then after many anxious weeks you were asked into the Science Club.

Fourth grade gave you a challenge you'd never had before and you came through scholastically with flying colors. How you loved it. On the recommendation of many of your teachers, you were given an IQ test, and on the basis of the results, your card was put into a "gifted child" file so that you'd be given the advantage of any advanced work or opportunity that Wightman has to offer.

During the year you took swimming lessons at Chatham on Saturday mornings and Oceanography at Buhl Planetarium at noon Saturdays. This summer you took Air Travel at the Planetarium—a course which you had recommended—and at the end of the course you were recommended by your instructor to receive an award as top student in your class…

September 4, 1962

We went to Jennerstown with the Brodies again this
year and once again you had a wonderful time. We all did!

You got your English Racer bike a week before your
birthday and riding it became a passionate love. Your first
"bike hike" with Jack Twersky you went to the News
Stand, to Schenley Park for a picnic lunch, to the Webster
Hall for a Coke. Then last week—on bikes—you took
Andi Brodie and Mavis Shure to lunch. I only found out
you had asked them when you asked me the night before
the rules of tipping. We explained the 15 to 20% rule, but
said that 10% would be fine for you to leave. The next
day you took them first to the Nature Museum in Schenley
Park. In the meantime I called Webster Hall so that no
one would challenge you on whether you had the money to

pay for lunch. I also explained that I suggested you sit at the counter so as not to tie up a table at their busy time. When the three of you entered Webster Hall, the hostess asked if you were Mead Mulvihill, and upon getting an affirmative answer, said that your mother had suggested you sit at the counter. Your reply was, "We'd prefer a table!" And you were then escorted to one. Your check came to $4.16 and you left a 40 cent tip. This was all your own money and you came home feeling like a king.

For your birthday we let you take David, Nickie Lauer, Jack Twersky and Stuart Shapiro to the Pirate game. "Lucky you" won a prize—a record, "The Fabulous Pirates."

I almost forgot, you also got to go to Philadelphia with your Dad right at the beginning of the summer. You saw the Liberty Bell, the Pennsylvania Superior Court in action, ate in an Automat and stayed in a luxurious hotel. You loved every minute of it but your dad was in his absolute glory. He was terribly proud and pleased to have you with him.

You make a wonderful "only child" but the din and confusion that exists when the four of you are together is sometimes quite maddening. I've had a particularly difficult summer with you. Sometimes, in my saner moments, I realize I'm frequently too hard on you, but I guess I just know your potential and don't want you to be any less than perfect. Unfortunately this is pretty tough on both of us at times.

You're a great guy, honey, and I hope, if I push too hard, that you'll understand it's because I love you dearly. You have one of the quickest and brightest little minds I've ever encountered in anyone. I'd love to know what your IQ is. I know it's over 135 because you were eligible for a "gifted child" session in Science at Falk this summer. You were very keen on it until you found out you'd have to take creative dramatics along with science. You then gave up the idea of summer school.

Fifth grade finds you once again in the advanced class. You've received an invitation to the Tam-O-Shanter art course at Carnegie Institute at 8:15 Saturday mornings. Much to my surprise, you're going—along with Mavis Shure, Helen Berkman and Cathy Copetas. You've given up a Magic class at the Arts and Crafts Center which conflicts with the art course. At 11 a.m. on Saturdays, you'll have swimming at Chatham.

You're slated to be busy but you're really happiest when you are that way.

Recently you were asked to be a school guard and you burst with pride. I'm still not _really_ keen on the idea but we'll see what happens.

To sum up—you are quite a guy. Daddy and I are very proud of you and love you very much. Stay as you are—only growing and advancing in character and personality as you have been. You'll be quite a man.

Love,
Mom

"We love you—and what's more we like you.
We'd be proud of you even if you weren't ours.
But we're grateful that you are—
very, very grateful."

August, 1963

Dear Mead,

World events of the past year like the impassioned fight of the Negroes for equal rights, the crack in relations between Russia and Red China, our boy Cooper's successful flight and the casualness with which he accomplished it, Russia's and the world's first lady astronaut—all of these important events are dimmed by the two weeks we are now enjoying at Nags Head—Kill Devil Hills, to be more precise, with the Brodies and Mallingers.

The trip down was lovely—all four of you children behaved perfectly. It was also my first trip into the South and I was fascinated and thrilled—as you were—by the historical places we passed through. We planned a stop in

Charlottesville to visit Monticello. It was all that everyone had led us to believe it was. I was awed by being in the home that once housed such a vibrant, intelligent, ingenious man.

Nags Head—or Kill Devil Hill, where we actually are—has captivated all of us. It's a sightseer's paradise. We were thrilled by the Wright Brothers Memorial, where we stood on the very ground where the "first flight" was accomplished. Our hearts throbbed faster each time a plane—be it a small, cozy Cessna or a high speed jet—waggled its wings over the Memorial in tribute to these men who helped make their flying possible.

We visited Fort Raleigh where the English first made an attempt to set up a colony in the virgin country. Later you went back to see "The Last Colony," a play which dramatized these efforts. We walked along the nature trail and found out the various local bushes and trees and learned to what use the colonists first put them.

We took our car on the Oregon Inlet ferry across to Cape Hatteras. The sea gulls gracefully swooped low and the sight of it all was sheer poetry.

On that trip we visited the Rodanthe fishing pier and saw the shipwreck of an old tanker. The feeling these old shipwrecks produce is something that I'm not capable of describing. We had lunch at the pier and then pushed on along miles and miles of desolate coastline until we reached the Cape Hatteras lighthouse. Daddy stayed at the bottom with Susie but the rest of us puffed our way to the top. (At least I puffed, it didn't seem to faze you three boys.) The view from the top was spectacular. The Pamlico Sound on one side, the Atlantic, with the famed Diamond Shoals, on the other. Another ferry ride, another shipwreck, and six tired people reached the cottage—having completed another perfect day.

Thirteen out of fourteen days brought us beautiful weather. That fourteenth day was also a beautiful day and one long to be remembered. The winds were fierce, but the natives didn't seem to be concerned so we weren't either. We drove down to Oregon Inlet to see the fishing boats come in. On the way, we passed the largest sand dune in the country and with the hurricane-like winds whipping the sand around, it was the eeriest sight we've ever seen. Again at the inlet, the terrific winds, the stalwart sea gulls, and the docking boats presented a panorama that was breathtaking.

Two days later we accepted the challenge or call of the dunes and went duning. It wasn't nearly as difficult as we thought it would be, but it <u>was</u> a thousand times more fun than we dreamed. From the top of the dunes, too, the *view was awesome.*

The walks on the beach, flying kites and model airplanes there, the hospitable people, the pleasant company—all of these things, and more, have not been mentioned, but all combined to give us a vacation that I think it's impossible to forget. The only thing wrong is— there just aren't enough superlatives to describe North Carolina's Outer Banks.

Tomorrow, sadly, we leave here to go to Williamsburg for a day of sightseeing, but we take with us a treasury of happy, happy memories.

"Last week you spoke of authoring a book,
but I don't think you've gotten to work on that yet."

September 4, 1963

As promised, a trip to Williamsburg followed Nags Head. We arrived in Williamsburg at 10:15—in time for the Plantation breakfast at the Williamsburg Inn. How super sensational it was! It got my vote as the highlight of the trip.

After breakfast we went to the tourist center to see the movie. It was a beautiful movie. After that we started our sightseeing trip in a town whose past, brilliant history immediately engulfs the tourist. It was quite an interesting day.

The trip home was nine hours worth of good roads and good fun.

But lest your accomplishments be lost in this travelogue I go back now to your past year.

The childhood diseases finally caught up with you. On January 30th, you fell victim to the mumps and before they had gone, you got a lovely case of measles. As usual, you were a great patient. Back to school for a few days and then you broke out in the worst case of hives I've ever seen. In all it was the unhealthiest year you've ever had. Because of this you can't return to the Tam-O-Shanter Art Classes, which you really came to love toward the end of the year. But the maximum number of absences permitted was four and you were absent ten times.

You accepted the responsibility of being a school guard like a man. Every day you were on duty, you got up, dressed, and were eating breakfast by the time I got up. By eight or ten after, you were on your way to school—and all this during the coldest winter we've had in a century. It paid off handsomely tho'. At the end of the school year you and Tommy Rosensweet were elected by the boys to be this year's Captains. It brings with it a weekend at Camp Kon-

O-Kwee coming up this September 13th.

This year has brought another large "privilege" to you. You're now old enough to play golf at Schenley. Your partners are usually Jay Cohen, Jeff Levinson, or Stuart Shapiro. You look like a "natural" and I think this is the beginning of a large love affair between you and the links.

Science and reading are still two of your favorite hobbies. Also swimming and golf are favorites. Others— not quite so important but still fun—include: tennis, baseball, football, model airplanes and collecting coins. Last week you spoke of authoring a book, but I don't think you've gotten to work on that yet.

Mavis and Andi are still your favorite girl people. Nicky Lauer and Gary Walk are your favorite boy people—other than Dave, Bob and Susie, of course.

David still doesn't realize completely—but I think

he's starting to get an inkling—how great a brother you are to him. Of course, there are many feuds, but underneath it all lies a very strong fondness for each other. Other mothers are openly envious about how well you two get along.

You're a much more responsible person this year than you've ever been. I think some good old-fashioned common sense is beginning to find a place in your make-up. Since we've returned from Nags Head we let you and Dave babysit while we go to Brodies or Mallingers or Rulins, etc. You've done a fine job. You also help with Susie in her "pottying" and have really become a huge help to me by clearing the table, etc.

Your grades continue to be great and your enthusiasm for learning is tops. We're really quite proud of you. We love you—and what's more we like you.

We'd be proud of you even if you weren't ours. But we're grateful that you are—very, very grateful.

> Love,
> Mom

Letter from Mead to
The Honorable Joseph S. Clark
US Senator

Mead J. Mulvihill III, 5470 Fair Oaks Street
Pittsburgh, PA 15217

April 15, 1964

The Honorable Joseph S. Clark,

   I think the Negroes have taken the kind of
treatment they get long enough. Although the Constitution
of the United States declares that all men are created
equal, some people seem to think that it really says all
men are created equal except negroes.

Mead J. Mulvihill III

"We've told David about Santa and fortunately he has you as an example so that he won't spoil Christmas for Bob and Susie. Like a good, good sport once again this year you stood in line with Susie to see Santa and put in a request. You're just great."

August 18, 1964

Dearest Mead,

    Five days ago in a lovely little spot called Elberon the Brodies entertained you on your twelfth birthday. It was lovely—in your words, "the best birthday ever."

    Much has happened since we celebrated your eleventh birthday. In November of '63 our beloved Val died. The sadness you felt was very great—the sobs came from ten years of loving our pooch. A few weeks later John Fitzgerald Kennedy was assassinated. At first you wouldn't watch TV and I thought you didn't have too much interest, but you said you were trying to forget because to know it made you too sad. But then you succumbed and watched it, as we did, almost every waking moment.

But life goes on, and just as we were beginning to smile again, we got the news that our favorite people, the Brodies, were leaving Pittsburgh to live in Elberon, New Jersey. We were sad then and we still miss them. I think they'll always be our good friends.

Your school year was another good one. As Captain of the Patrol Guards you acquired a sense of responsibility and a sense of confidence you'd never had before. You seemed to grow up into a young man right before our eyes.

You appeared on television with three or four other students and Henry Koerner to discuss the art collection at Wightman.

In the Christmas program, I gasped at the beauty of the sixth grade's participation.

But when you opened the French program at the end of the school year and then sang solo, I was astonished and quite proud of the great job you did.

Your interests are as wide and varied as the world. Reading, studying, golf and swimming head the list. Daddy claims you're going to be a great golfer. The only thing that I know of that does distress you quite a bit is that it's becoming increasingly obvious that you're going to have to learn to dance and you don't think you want to. It's sad and our heart aches for you, but I guess it's a part of growing up we all have to do.

Generally—about 98% of the time—you're a reasonable, happy, easy-going guy. Sometimes, like the first week after school let out, you were impossibly difficult to live with. I didn't know what was wrong with you and neither did you. But as Daddy pointed out, it was a large dose of growing-up-itis. I'm happy to report that you've fully recovered and are once again a joy to have around.

Ten days before we were scheduled to go on vacation Granddaddy O'Brien had a heart attack. He's still not well by a long shot, but hopefully he's on the mend. While I made trips to the hospital you were a brick in keeping things going smoothly with Dave, Bob and Susie. I was proud of all of you and extremely grateful.

Since things were going pretty well with Granddaddy we proceeded with our vacation as planned. We spent a glorious week in Lavallette, N. J. with several meetings in Elberon with the Brodies and a short visit to Atlantic City to view the Boardwalk and Daddy's old cottages and Convention Hall where the networks were setting up for next week's Democratic convention. You had a brief flare up with a tummy virus while there which did you out of a dinner at the Traymore Coffee Shop. After a dose of some hastily purchased medicine, you recovered in time to buy souvenirs and saltwater taffy before we left.

Our historical side trip this year was to Gettysburg and we all enjoyed it tremendously. You and David have become real Civil War buffs as a result. We were all most anxious to get a picture of you and Daddy by General Meade's statue. Apparently Gen. Meade was a friend of J. P. Mulvihill's father (your great great grandfather), and Pop Mulvihill was named James Meade Mulvihill in honor of that friendship. Pop later dropped the "e" from Meade and legally changed his name to Mead James.

Your best friends are Nicky Lauer and Bobby Finkelhor. On the girl side of the ledger it's still Mavis and

Andi. I think your favorite companion, tho', is David. Going to Allderdice this year may keep you apart more and give Dave a chance to develop his own friends a little more than he has in the past. You're absolutely great with younger children.

Love,
Mom

December 7, 1964

Dear Mead,

More impressions, three and a half months later.
Like the obstinate perfectionist you've always been, you
finally learned to dance. It all happened about six weeks
ago. It was agonizing torment for you, and in the end, we
all had to learn the Frug. But by the time Andi arrived
from Elberon at the end of October, you had mastered
that illusive mystery of learning "the dance." I'm proud—
we're proud—terribly proud of you.

You've loved Allderdice from the beginning. You
made the honor roll on the first report—just barely. And
we hope that tomorrow when you get your second report
you'll have gone up a little more in points.

119

We've told David about Santa and fortunately he has you as an example so that he won't spoil Christmas for Bob and Susie. Like a good, good sport once again this year you stood in line with Susie to see Santa and put in a request. You're just great.

Right now you're a bit of a hypochondriac. I guess that's normal at your age—or so I'm told. It must be an age of many insecure times, many terrible moments of realizing we're all mortal. We know you'll outgrow it, but, gads, sometimes its difficult.

That's my only complaint—and what a small one in the large scheme of things. You're a bright, logical, reasonable guy. You're affectionate and loving and a very nice little fellow. (Did I say "little"—you're only three inches shorter than I am now.)

Grow in wisdom, dear son, you have tremendous potential.

We love you,
Mom

"Your scholastic grades indicate an obvious ability in the sciences. But you also have a beautifully logical mind and are developing a strong sense of diplomacy and tact. You have always been the most 'responsible' child I've ever encountered."

August 14, 1965

Dear Mead,

Right now we're approaching the Breezewood exit of the Pennsylvania Turnpike on our way to meet the Mallingers at Rehoboth Beach, Delaware. After that we'll meet the Rulins in Madison-on-the-Lake, Ohio. So for two weeks we'll be in vacation-land away from the problems of Viet Nam, the cold war, the thought that in six years you'll be of draft age.

Yesterday, on Friday 13th, you celebrated your 13th birthday. It's been a great year for you. In school, you made the honor roll each report—sometimes the high honor roll. You easily made it into the Scholars program and elected to

start a four year Latin program this September. In your
final exams you had the top score in the advanced class in
Math. You finished Science with an A+ average. Pretty
good for a young squirt (excuse the obvious pride).

This summer we joined the Bel Air swim club and
it's made it a lovely summer. You and David have played
quite a bit of tennis, but you've both concentrated mainly
on your swimming. David managed to pass his Beginner,
Advanced Beginner and Intermediate tests before leaving
for Rehoboth. You proudly sport a "Swimmer" patch on
your bathing trunks. It was tough to come by, but I'm
certain you felt ten feet tall when it was placed in your
hands. It was a reward you really deserved.

After completing the regular test for Bob this past
Wednesday you were tested by Jack Morris on Thursday. He

tied your hands together and your feet together and had you swim several widths of the pool. It was a sight to behold. You did it as gracefully as if you'd been doing it all your life while I watched with my heart in my mouth. Even the lifeguards were fascinated by the performance. Rick was so shocked he removed his shoes—a feat in itself—to make Rick come to life. After that you swam 36 lengths of the pool (by your count—40, by ours) and then you were handed the coveted "Swimmer" badge. It was a spectacular performance.

Since last summer you've also become quite accomplished with the guitar. Dave Bergholz has done a good job as teacher and you've obviously been a fair-to-middlin' student. It's a happy sound to hear you up in your room singing and playing "Puff the Magic Dragon" or "Go Tell It On the Mountain." As soon as Susie hears you she rushes up the steps to join the chorus.

You have a favorite new game, "Wff 'n Poof"—a game slightly more complicated than chess. You also enjoy playing cards, doing crossword puzzles, playing golf, and gathering facts. You stun me with the amount of knowledge you possess.

A hero of mine—Adlai Stevenson—died recently. I hope he becomes a hero of yours, too, because you possess many of the fine qualities of this great man. There's no doubt that you will be equal to any profession you choose to enter. Your scholastic grades indicate an obvious ability in the sciences. But you also have a beautifully logical mind and are developing a strong sense of diplomacy and tact. You have always been the most "responsible" child I've ever encountered. You are also the most technical child I've ever seen, and I hope your wife will be smart enough to develop the same "shrug the shoulder" attitude I have developed to enable me to live with you and your father. Sometimes I have to grit my teeth a little too, but you're both such sweet guys that it's worth the effort.

"In closing, I must sum up that you're a real teenager now with all the confusing, perplexing problems that confront a teen, but with an above average ability to cope with these problems. We're extraordinarily proud of you."

December 7, 1965

Dear Mead,

A slight lapse in time, but having taken over the presidency of the Wightman P.T.A., it's been hectic.

You've done very well so far in school with—surprise of surprises—Latin and English taking over as your favorite subjects. I suppose thanks for this must go to a couple of fabulous teachers—Mr. Welling in English and Mr. Audia in Latin.

A little over a month ago, you were one of twenty scholars chosen from the entire city's Scholar program (one of three from Allderdice) to take a Fine Arts Experimental Course at Carnegie Tech—you love it!!!

Today you, Nicky Lauer, Martha Schafer and

Allison Loercky conducted the Swift Experiment in eyewitness testimony in your Social Studies class. It apparently went over very well. I was pleased that you took the initiative in proving your theory.

In addition to guitar, games, etc., you have added to your list of hobbies with a passionate interest in coin collecting.

In closing, I must sum up that you're a real teenager now with all the confusing, perplexing problems that confront a teen, but with an above average ability to cope with these problems. We're extraordinarily proud of you.

Happy Birthday and Merry Christmas.

We love you,
Mom

September 1, 1966

My dear Mead,

I fit right into the era—as you can see by the above date, I'm somewhat disorganized this summer. Bel Air tends to make one somewhat lazy.

The world is in something of a chaotic state—the war in Viet Nam continues, the civil rights issue now competes with the national economy as our number one domestic problem. And, with each passing year, you are more aware of these problems.

Your year at Allderdice was an exceptionally good one. You were one of those chosen to take the County Algebra test given by the Math Society. You were almost chosen to take the County Latin test, but on a "flip of the coin" type situation you lost out, but will probably be the student to take it this year. You staged a "mock crime" in Social Studies to prove to the teacher that eyewitness testimony is not too reliable. You had the finest English teacher I've ever heard of, but even he learned from you. He discovered your logic book, <u>Clear Thinking</u>, and it is currently being used as a guide in preparing a tenth grade course. Since Mr. Welling is now an exchange teacher in England, Lord only knows when we'll get our book back. You were chosen to take an experimental Fine Arts course at Carnegie Tech on Saturday mornings. Though it meant getting up early and walking there you enjoyed it tremendously. Since this was sponsored by a Foundation, you got an extra bonus at the end of the year—traveling money. Since you walked, it was $16.00 "in the clear" for you.

You took a Junior Life Saving course at Bel Air

this summer and the evening of the last lesson you were involved in an automobile accident on the way home with the Lazarus'. Though both Mrs. Lazarus and Bruce were hurt, you were in your "safety seat" (right rear), and except for a slight bump on your leg, escaped without any injury. You took the Junior Life Saving test the next morning and scored 58 out of a possible 60 points. So far no one has any higher, though two have tied you.

An old hobby has suddenly become an intense pastime with you—coin collecting. You and David and Bobby haven't spent a penny on anything but coins. Your collections are all coming along beautifully. Our current sport is racing back and forth to the bank for rolls of nickels and pennies.

You're still an avid reader and a passionate student— of everything. Even the stock market—which is in a crazy

133

decline—has caught your eye. When the time is right, we've told you that you can take some money out of your savings account and buy into one of the mutual funds.

You're still something of a dreamer, not always down to earth. You'd rather sort coins than bowl, rather read than earn money washing cars or shoveling snow. Your circle of friends is exclusive—chosen with care. Ricky Finkel, Nicky Lauer and a new swimming friend, Milton Gurin, are probably your favorites. However, you've learned to meet new people and new situations with confidence. You're conservative in dress and actions— always neat and always proper. You're really a model son—handsome, intelligent and completely trustworthy.

Love,
Mom

September 7, 1966

Dear Mead,

What's to become of you? Well, your interests are so varied that you'd fit right into many careers—law, medicine, teaching—to name just a few. You're strong in Math, Logic, Science and History. On the other hand, you're creative enough to do quite well in English and the arts. You found out yesterday that you'll continue in Project Fine Arts on Saturday mornings this year at Tech. We shall see!

You are still adamant, though, that you will attend the University of Pittsburgh—no out-of-state school for you. I wonder if this is really your choice or if you're patterning *your life after your father's. You are most definitely like him in almost all ways and I'm sure this is deliberate on your part. You love and respect him very much and want to be like him. You've chosen a good model.*

You're a good boy—I hope the sun shines upon the rest of the world and gives it the brilliance that you and many of your generation already possess. You are quite literally the future of our world.

We love you,
Mom

July 24, 1967

My dear Mead,

Your fifteenth birthday is just around the corner, and in many ways, you know the score. You know that "war" isn't a fun game played by tousled-headed, happily grimy little boys. You know that "war" is a hideous thing that could in a few years involve you.

You're a very bright, mature young man, but often you slip back to a delightfully giddy stage known as "childhood." In many ways you're quite sophisticated but in many things you retain a childlike innocence....

"You're really a perfect all-round boy and if I seem to lose patience with you when you go off on cloud nine away from us mortals, it's only because you've led me to expect the most and best from you."

August 10, 1967

You know all of the chaotic things going on in the world, you understand the silver market and the implications of the riots and the need for equality for all, but how to cope with boy-girl relationships is a little more difficult. You handle them like most fifteen year old boys always have. Daddy and I have a feeling that your heart will be broken many times because you're inclined to feel strongly about one gal at a time.

You are still a sensational student—finishing ninth grade with A's in everything but gym. You crave knowledge and soak it up like a dry sponge soaks up water. You had several excellent teachers this year. Mr. Herman, your Biology teacher, was your favorite. But Mrs. Thurmond (English) and Mr. Audia (Latin) were close seconds.

Practically all of your teachers took the time to write "excellent student" on your final report. Mrs. Thurmond really sent you up to cloud nine by calling one evening to compliment you on a project that she thought was brilliant.

Socially you've advanced, too. Poker games were the order of business each weekend. Ricky Finkel is one of your closest friends. You walk home from school together and then get together after school to play ball or cards or what have you. You also share a common passion—coin collecting. You've spent a fortune this summer buying coins. When we went to Jennerstown on vacation this summer, you spent all of your money in the antique shops buying coins. Then, in New Jersey, Pearl Brodie led you to a coin shop that was going out of business and you bought more coins. Your collection is fantastic and you have it completely catalogued and in perfect order.

*You're an easy child to have around the house—
capable of amusing yourself not just for hours, but days and
weeks at a time. You're an avid reader, game player and
card player. You're pretty darn good at card tricks. You still
love playing golf, though you can't wait until next year when
you don't have to play on children's day. You also still pick
up your guitar every so often to keep a hand in on that.*

*You're really a perfect all-round boy and if I seem
to lose patience with you when you go off on cloud nine
away from us mortals, it's only because you've led me to
expect the most and best from you. Of course that's not
completely reasonable—who said mothers have to be
reasonable! Just keep your sense of humor and everything
will work out fine.*

*The lines of communication are open in our
house—at least we hope they are. You and the rest of the*

kids seem to feel free to discuss any and all subjects with us. I hope it always remains the same. We seem to have something very special in our house at 5470 Fair Oaks—I hope that Dad and I aren't deluding ourselves, but we feel love and respect and peace surrounding us. It's kind of comforting to feel that in this hustling chaotic world there's an island of tranquility. It's been good for us as parents, and we hope that you children have found it the same.

For me there is still only one measure of success— what kind of person you are. I think you stand a good chance of being one of the most successful of all time. You're a great guy and we love you very much.

Grow straight and tall and have faith in people. There's good in all—sometimes we not only have to find it, we have to help them find it. God save you from war and violence and make your life as happy as ours has been.

Happy Birthday.

> *Love,*
> *Mother*

P. S. Lest we forget—and I find it difficult to believe that any of us could—I would like to chronicle our recent trip to New York City.

On July 28th we took a TWA jet. It was the first jet flight for me and the four children. It was a miserable day here and in New York so we did nothing on Friday except get ready for our big evening at Les and Fan's. (We stayed at Don and Leslie's charming apartment at 155 E. 50th St.)

At 6:15, the doorman buzzed us to tell us the limousine had arrived. Uncle Les' chauffeur held the door of the most beautiful Lincoln Continental any of us had ever seen. It impressed David more than anything else on the trip. In the back, the seats faced each other and there was a walnut console which housed a hi-fi, bar, etc.

Cronin, the butler, ushered us in at 666 Park and then the fun began. There was a beautifully wrapped package for each one of us. We were taken in shifts up to visit Aunt Fan who had suffered a slight stroke a month or so before. She and Les were absolutely charming, and as usual, the perfect hosts.

For dinner we had shrimp and crab aspic (in the shape of a fish) surrounded by a blue frill of seafood paste (probably roe). They used a simple table setting in deference to you children and a perfect children's dinner: steak, french fries, french fried onions, green beans and dinner rolls. You were permitted a little sauterne with the aspic and a little burgundy with the main course. You all

144

handled the finger bowl and doily like pros. And then came a heavenly chocolate mousse with chocolate sauce and little cake squares. Those of you who wished had a little demitasse after dinner.

In addition to the beautiful floral centerpiece, there were dishes of extraordinary nuts on the table and various colored, foil-wrapped dried fruits for each of you children.

After a hasty trip to the elegant brown satin-walled and gold-fixtured powder room (Susie, particularly, flipped), the limousine took us to the theatre where we saw (from the 6th and 11th row center) "Fiddler On the Roof" with Hershel Bernardi. The four of you loved it, but Daddy and I have never seen anything we loved as much. It was brilliant.

The Lincoln was waiting for us directly in front of the theatre and people bent over and gaped inside to see if it was a celebrity's car. We were taken back to East 50th Street but we had just experienced an evening none of us will soon forget. It was delicious.

The next day we had lunch with Mike Held at the "Flick," a charming place, and then had tickets for Radio City Music Hall. All of this was great fun, but sort of an anticlimax after the night before.

On to New Jersey the next day, and, by your own admission, this was your favorite part of the trip. But how could Park Avenue ever compare to the Brodies, or more particularly, Andi Brodie?!! Ah youth! But we all agree—it was a fun four days and hope we can do it again soon!

Love,
Mom

Dear Dave,

What a hideous nightmare we've all been through. Your dear brother, your best friend, died on December 30, 1967 at 11:50 p.m.

We were all anxiously awaiting the arrival of the Brodies on the 28th. They arrived in time for dinner. Mead, who was so enthusiastic about spending the holiday with Andi, was absolutely beside himself with joy. All of their friends arrived—the adults in the living room, the older kids in the dining room and Claudia, Bobby and Susie upstairs. Around ten-thirty, Mead went upstairs, not feeling well. I was sure it was excitement and that he would be fine by morning, I made his apologies downstairs.

The next morning he was feeling worse and had a fever of 104°. The doctor wasn't upset because the bug was going around. Late Friday there was no improvement and by Saturday morning it was obvious that he was really quite a sick young man. Daddy reached Dr. Bass at the office and told him it was "urgent"—a word we've never used before to a doctor. He came right out, called the police ambulance and off we went to Children's Hospital. The x-ray showed it was pneumonia and I was relieved because pneumonia can be treated. Little did we know!

He was put through a series of tests and was so good that I promised him a 32 D or S quarter as soon as the coin shops opened on Tuesday. He kept rambling on about his "quarter" all day. He even made light by saying, "Comics first—first section first; second section second," a joke between the two of you about the Sunday funnies.

At about 4:50 they took him to Presbyterian Hospital for a brain scan—just another test to eliminate any other problem. They had just finished the first part of the test at 5:50 when Mead's heart stopped. The "STAT" call went over the hospital loudspeaker. I've been around hospitals long enough to know what happens next. I had heard Mead mumble his last word and then the technician's frantic plea, "Mead—Mead" before she sounded the "STAT" alarm and started mouth-to-mouth resuscitation.

I knew the doors to the Radio-Isotope section were locked so I quickly raced to hold it open for the emergency team. When the last doctor went through, a kindly nurse led me to a chair in the waiting room. Jerry Wolfson came innocently upon the scene and trembled with compassion. I told him I had called Bass' already and that Lee and Daddy were on their way. Then I sent him back to help Meadie. He came out a few minutes later—Meadie was breathing on his own again. I stopped smoking—I tried to make a deal with God—Mead's life and regardless of ulcer or anything else—I'd never smoke again. About 7:30 we were heartened by the news that Mead, though still unconscious, had better color. But even then he didn't have a chance. His lungs were almost completely destroyed by a combination of bi-lateral viral pneumonia and a staph infection. At 11:50—he died.

He hadn't known undue fear and he hadn't suffered—for that I'll be eternally grateful...

When we went to the funeral home the next day, your grief was almost too much to bear. You had me slip your favorite silver dollar into Mead's breast pocket to be with him always. You put your hand over his and sobbed as if your heart would break.

Later Daddy put his favorite gargoyle tie clasp on Mead. I couldn't decide what to give him, when finally Monday night I decided on a note (since I'm forever writing letters to you children, it seemed appropriate to me) which I placed with him before the funeral service on Tuesday. You didn't seem terribly pleased by my "gift" but I think someday later you'll understand...

Letter placed in Mead's coffin

January 2, 1968

My dear, dear Mead,

You were handsome and so very, very bright—but most of all you were extraordinarily good.

You've given us fifteen and a half years of joy and happiness and great pride and we love you.

Daddy, David, Bobby and Susie join me in saying that we love you and we miss you so much already that we ache. You'll always live in all of our hearts and minds.

Sleep peacefully, my son.

With love and undying affection,
Mother

"To live in hearts we leave behind—is not to die."

—*Thomas Campbell*

Peggy Mulvihill has continued writing birthday letters to Mead since his death in 1967. Following are some of these letters.

April 18, 1968
(on way to Brodies')

Somehow it's different—We try to pretend it's not so.

*The Cheerios were consumed—The car Tic-Tac-Toe is
being played—We're packed and moving but the usual
excitement is dulled by heavy hearts.*

One of us is missing—and always will be—though

He will forever be our silent hitchhiker…

With us each moment—each second of each day.

Our thoughts, actions and deeds forever influenced by him.

We swallow the tears—or try to—a few escape.

*This was a trip—these pilgrimages to the Brodies—that he
loved most of all.*

157

Now I must pull the curtain—try to shut out for a time—
the memories of the not-so-long-ago—lest the tears and
the pain push us over the brink.

The hills are the same, the view is the same—

Only we are different.

Pax Vobiscum. Amen.

August 13, 1977
70 degrees—cloudy, gray

Once this was a day of laughter and festivities—airplane parties, pirate parties, cowboy parties—days of balloons and ice cream and fantastic cakes and friends and favors and deliciously happy moments.

Today on a hillside—a dozen white Carnations and an enchanting ladybug pay homage to a light that is bright in our memories.

Happy 25th, dear Mead—you live in our hearts!

The curtain of clouds was pulled back long enough tonight to expose one bright, breathtaking shooting star. Golden-orange, it shot across the sky over my head as I lay on the deck chair. A fitting ending to August 13th.

August 13, 1982
72 degrees, blue sky, puffy clouds

Dear Meadie,

We had you for fifteen years…We've been without you for fifteen years. You are still alive in our hearts and minds!

The solemnity of the "student"—soaking up facts and philosophies like the proverbial sponge…

The mischievous bent of the "child"—teasing mother, flying balsa wood airplanes or real ones with Dad…

The tenacity of the "learner"—perfecting skills in private before you would try them out in public…

The sensitivity and love of the "son and brother"— letting the smaller boys tag along to ball games, protecting

161

Susie from those same boys' teasing, the spoken gratitude to parents for little things.

You were all of these and much, much more!

On that gently sloping hill in Pittsburgh, Susie and Bobby today placed red Carnations from the florist in Jenner, mixed with Queen Anne's Lace from the roadside in Jennerstown.

Tonight we celebrated your birthday with Mindy and David at the Green Gables. It was an enchanting, sentimental evening.

Richard Finkel called before we left for the Gables. He, too, remembers the "friend."

God be with you!

Love,
Mom

August 13, 1985

Time flies on wings of seconds, minutes, years!
When I was thirty-three years old, my fourth—
and youngest child—was two years old. I was a woman!
I think of you still, dear Mead—our first born—as my
little boy!

In Pittsburgh, a bouquet of white Mums decorates
your resting place. Late last night, in Jennerstown, Susie
and I—in your memory—watched the shooting stars.
How wonderful to have such a clear, crisp, wonderful
night to lie on the dock and cast our eyes toward Heaven.
There were giggly moments—there were philosophical
moments. It brought back memories of a young lad on a
porch in Nags Head, celebrating his 13th birthday to the

awesome spectacle of the Perseid shower of stars dancing over the Atlantic Ocean. What a smashing show!—What a special young lad !!

   Our hearts—for all time—are with you!

August 13, 1986
69 degrees

China blue skies, sunny day, some clouds

"Catch a shooting star and treasure it forever."

On the slopes at Calvary, Daisies and Queen Anne's Lace honor your memory—stand as a tribute to the happy times we shared with you.

Last night, Bob, Susie and I made a symbolic pilgrimage to the dock to watch the Perseid Shower of Stars. Our teeth chattered from the chilly night air, but we were rewarded with the sightings of several shooting stars.

Fog moved gracefully across the lake—Susie and I giggled about how cold it was—Bob chided us that we were interrupting the solemnity of the night. We were *celebrating you and your upcoming birthday. Tonight we continue the celebration with dinner at the Gables.*

Pax Vobiscum!

August 13, 1987

cool nights, warm, sunny days

Life is so fragile—each moment is so precious!

Purple Statice and lemon leaves mark your grave, dear Mead. Gone from us for almost twenty years, you live in our lives in a very forceful way.

Young men die…Old women know those young men have been cheated. It makes the sense of loss all the more poignant. It reminds us that each moment, each opportunity for a memory is a very special thing. Our time with you was extraordinary—you gave us many wonderful memories which we cherish.

From our hearts and souls, we send you love!

August 13, 1988
In Pittsburgh

How appropriate that the Perseid Shower of Stars occurs every year at this time. You—our comet—are personified by every glimmering, golden streak that rides across the heavens! Twenty-one years after your death, the aura of your life remains with us in a very personal, loving way.

It is the hottest summer on record since 1881. By Summer's end, it <u>will be</u> the hottest summer on record…too hot even to venture to the mountains. So— we celebrate your birthday in Pittsburgh.

Eucalyptus, purple and white Mums decorate your grave. A handful of seed invites the birds to visit you, too.

Bob, Susie, John and Steffi called—because it is today and you are remembered…and you are loved.

Pax Vobiscum, dear son!

August 13, 1988
94 degrees very hot, very humid

The Falling Star
by Sara Teasdale

I saw a star slide down the sky,
Blinding the north as it went by,
Too burning and too quick to hold,
Too lovely to be bought or sold,
Good only to make wishes on
And then forever to be gone.

The skies here and in Jennerstown have been too
cloudy and hazy to see a star, much less a shooting star.

171

Though a little cloudy in Rochester, Susie and John "think" they saw one last night.

Dear Susie, tho', sent me a gold shooting star for my charm bracelet…a forever, loving remembrance.

11:15 p.m.

Susie and John have called twice—3 brilliant shooting stars—several lesser ones. John's hooked after his first sky searching experience.

August 13, 1989
In Pittsburgh

Amidst the Impatiens, Marigolds and Dusty Miller, white Daisies and miniature golden Asters mark your resting place on this quiet Sunday. With bird seed scattered around your grave, it's almost festive—in a poignant sort of way—for your 37th birthday.

For us, however, a sadness lingers on. Until the day we die, a part of our heart will grieve for the "what might have been"…will long for the bright, sweet character that was.

"Every man is a river that flows within every group of worshippers to the great sea of believers. Each

group of believers is a river running to the Great Source from which it came…"

from All Rivers Run to the Sea
—Joyce Hifler

August 13, 1990

In Pittsburgh

Cloudy—rain

It's 1990! There was a time when this day was a joyous one—filled with parties, gifts, friends, laughter and love.

It's difficult to believe that today you would be 38 years old—one year older than I was when you died. To me, you are still that same sweet, cheerful, inquisitive 15 year old planning chess strategies, solving chemical equations, reading voraciously.

The skies are cloudy, so not even Bob can search the skies for shooting stars. No matter!—The dear little sister whom you loved so much sent us a card—filled with silver stars and hot pink hearts. The card said:

"Mom and Dad

Thinking of you
and a little boy
Who believed poplar trees
were there for God
to sweep the sky"

You have never left us—you are part of our character—part of our hearts. We will love you forever.

P.S. Susie called at 11 p.m.—she had just seen a shooting star! Bravo!!!

P.P.S. Bob's dedication in his article published in The Auk, July 1990:

"Mulvihill dedicates this paper to the memory of Mead J. Mulvihill III, who was fascinated by science and flight."

August 13, 1991
86 degrees
sunny with increasing clouds

Thirty-nine years ago you came into our lives and changed the meaning of what life was about. To have a perfect little child—so fragile and wonderful—as part of our lives was, indeed, a miracle.

You were taken from us much too soon. We all continue to love you, to miss you and to be influenced by you. This year we have another small miracle—your namesake, Mead Samuel Mulvihill, born to Bob and Bonnie on December 28th, 1990. He guarantees that another generation will hold you close to its heart.

On a parched hillside at Calvary, Dad, Susie and

I placed a bouquet of Eucalyptus, Liatris and Star of Bethlehem. Your star shines brightly—never to be diminished in our lifetime.

August 13, 1992
73 degrees, gray, occasional rain

This week I copied each of my entries from August 13th, thinking that I would have 25 of them to present to your two brothers and your sister to mark that anniversary of your 40th birthday. Imagine my surprise when I discovered that for three years, on your birthday, I had not had the courage to address the reality of your death.

It's not recorded that David started a collection of pictures at Children's Hospital within a month of your death in your memory, starting with Charles Schulz "Peanuts" cartoon strips and building quickly through the years. It's not written that David hired an airplane and a pilot to fly him over your grave to give the flyers' waggle of the wings. It's not stated that Dad and I began a

179

research fund at Children's Hospital in your memory and that the Radiology Waiting Room now has a bronze plaque in it, also in your memory. These are the footsteps that we attempted to leave in the sand to give evidence to future generations that you lived and were loved and that your life was important and an inspiration to all of us.

We live in the present, but we remember that past with respect and love and happy memories. You were a star, so it's fitting that your birthday and you are celebrated during the annual Perseid Shower of Stars.

Crickets sang in the starless sky last night. A full moon and city lights hid the stars from our view. Today is gray and is giving us off-and-on showers. This afternoon, Dad and I will take yellow Daisies and Ruscus to Calvary—a token of love from the five you left behind.

We love you still!!!

August 21, 1992
76 degrees. Sunny—Beautiful

When we arrived home last Sunday, there was a Flavia card waiting for us from Susie—a plain blue card with an archway of stars. It said, "Perhaps what we had came from a star, and was a kind of magic, only ours to borrow for a while."

Inside Susie had written a poem. It was dated August 13, 1992 and I want to add it to this journal because it is so special…

A little boy
Who loved the sky
Ascends to Heaven
And the night does cry.
Stars, like teardrops
begin to fall

Messages from a child
So loved by all…
So bright
They take our breath away
Gone too soon
We wish it'd stay…
But beauty like that
While it makes the heart sing,
Is more precious because
It's an ephemeral thing.
So we wipe a tear
And send love afar
And wave at the brilliant
Shooting star…
"Surely, a star danced in Heaven on the day you was born," Flavia wrote…and the dance continues…

August 13, 1993

Friday, the thirteenth

"One runs the risk of weeping a little, if one lets himself be tamed."

> —The Little Prince, Antoine de Saint Exupery

Another year has rolled around and you, Mead, Prince of King Friday the 13th's Court, would be forty-one years old.

On the slope at Calvary, miniature burgundy and white Carnations mark your resting place. Our hearts are still heavy from our loss—our memories still alive of the extra special young man you were. It is with profound love and respect that we remember you—not just on this day, but on every day of the year.

183

The Perseid Shower this year is supposed to be one of the most spectacular of our time. Each night David, Bob, Susie and we have anxiously searched the sky. Alas, the heavens have been covered, not even a break the size of a postage stamp has appeared to give us a glimpse of this wonder. No matter—you are our star in the heavens—brighter than all of the Perseid Shower!

P. S. Susie had a star named in your honor at the Carnegie Science Center!

August 13, 1994
75 degrees at 8 a.m.
hot, humid, cloudy & gray

Once there was a young lad who, after your death, asked his parents what would happen to us (Mead's parents). They said that time would make us forget. Evan was visibly shaken that such a thing could happen. When I heard about it, I assured him that such a thing could never happen, that this time his parents were absolutely wrong. And they were! One never forgets a comet! Nor would one want to!!!

We have never forgotten the magnificence of you, the son...the brother...the friend. What a splendid member of the human race you were! To this day you influence us by who you were!

185

The Irish superstitious part of me likes to have a little rain on your birthday. At 4 o'clock this afternoon, a boomer of a storm, with torrential downpour, came through. I smiled for you!

Unfortunately, it looks like we won't be seeing any stars tonight. The skies show only clouds.

At your grave, on the slopes of Calvary, a bouquet of Zinnias from the garden of your sister-in-law, Liz, marks your resting place. When we leave tomorrow we're taking a bouquet of Hydrangeas and Cosmos from the garden of your other sister-in-law, Bonnie, directly to Calvary for you.

You remain an influential part of our lives.
We love you! Pax Vobiscum!

10:35 p.m. Susie excitedly reports shooting stars over Darien.

August 13, 1994

Another young man (23 years old) was recently buried at Calvary. His headstone is black marble, etched with the following well-known poem which is often quoted. We love its' sentiment.

> Do not stand at my grave and weep
> I am not there, I do not sleep
> I am a thousand winds that blow
> I am a diamond glint of snow
> I am the sunlight on ripened grain
> I am the gentle Autumn rain.
> When you awake in the morning hush I am
> the swift, uplifting rush
> Of quiet birds in circling flight

I am the soft starshine at night.
Do not stand by my grave and cry
I am not there....
　　　I did not die.

Acknowledgments—Peggy Mulvihill

I never thought for a moment that I had written a book. Since it turns out that I did, I would like to thank some very special people:

My husband, Mead, and our sons, David and Bob, overcame some early reluctance to help us proofread and have photos copied for the project. Their advice was invaluable.

The best son-in-law anyone ever had, John Parran, also pitched in with typing, proofreading and general kibitzing over the end project.

As for Susie, what can I say!?! She said that she'd get Mead's letters published and, by God, she did! She was determined to have the whole world know her brother. I am indebted to her for her sweetness, her love and her determination. She's a very special daughter and a very, very special sister. Mead would be especially proud of her!

Both Susie and I are indebted to Dominique Raccah and Todd Stocke from Sourcebooks. They have been a joy to work with. All first time authors should be so lucky.

Acknowledgments—Susie Mulvihill Parran

To my wonderful husband, John, for believing in me now, still, always. To Alicia Caufield, who by so generously transcribing the letters, proved she is "a friend indeed." To Cathe, Liche, Judy, Mel, Mindy, Wendi, Cindi, Molly and Beth, whom I can count on for support, humor and enthusiasm in all my ventures, but especially this one. To Ellen for helping me learn to trust my own instincts and persevere. To Fred Hetzel and Susan Elizabeth for their sound advice. To Flavia for her encouragement. To Roy Engelbrecht for a photo finish. To Betty for leading me to Sourcebooks. To Dominique and Todd for sharing my vision of what this book could be and for the immediate enthusiasm they showed for the project. To Wayne for a stellar cover..."Thank you!"

Thanks go, too, to my brothers, Bob and David, for permitting their little sister to go public with something that heretofore had been a private family story. To my father for always lovingly insisting that I could do and be anything I wanted. To my mother for teaching me that all things are possible and, of course, most especially, for allowing me to share these incredible letters.

And to our Angels in the outfield who watched over us and this project.

From an original linoleum print by
Mead J. Mulvihill III, 1952–1967

"...the thought has tickled my mind that the 11 year old boy who expressed a desire 'to author a book' has finally done it..."

—Susie Mulvihill Parran

About The Author

Peggy Mulvihill is a mother of four from Pittsburgh, PA. Her work for mayoral campaigns, the Pittsburgh Penguins, and several community and charity organizations have led her to become one of Pittsburgh's best-loved citizens. Susie Mulvihill Parran was the driving force behind Letters to Mead. Her determination to share the special gift of her mother's birthday letters has brought you this book.

Terrific Books for Your Family

365 Afterschool Activities
TV Free Fun for Kids Ages 7-12
by Sheila Ellison and Judith Gray
"Contains a wealth of engaging and fun-filled activities that are sure to keep kids playing, imagining and creating all year long."
— Brenda Pilson, Creative Classroom Magazine
ISBN: 1-57071-080-5; $12.95

365 Days of Creative Play
For Children 2 Years & Up
by Sheila Ellison and Judith Gray
"Activities that may work magic. Projects that you can do with your kids, and even better, activities they can do by themselves."
— Family Circle Magazine
ISBN: 1-57071-029-5; $12.95

365 Foods Kids Love to Eat
Fun, Nutritious and Kid-Tested
by Sheila Ellison and Judith Gray
"A boon to busy parents and hungry kids alike."
— Parenting Magazine
ISBN: 1-57071-030-9; $12.95

The '365' series of childcare books has been designed to make parenting less challenging and more fun. *They are available from your local bookseller or gift store*, or call Sourcebooks at (708) 961-3900.

To receive a catalog of Sourcebooks' publications, please write to us at:
P.O. Box 372
Naperville, IL 60566